Contents

Introduction

You probably think witches are just funny old ladies with pointy hats and broomsticks.

But no one with half a brain really believes in witches these days.

Witches make great stories but only an idiot believes a real person could fly on a broomstick…

And only a real twit would think a witch could put a spell on you.

So how can you have a history book about people who don't exist? The thing is, people USED to believe in witches.

People have always believed in 'magic' – invisible forces that can be very useful if only you can control them. Someone who thought magic worked for them became known as a 'witch'. Even if the 'magic' they used was a cure for a spot on your nose made from herbs.

The Bible says…

You should not allow a witch to live.

And that led to a lot of cruelty, stupidity and horror.

If you had a handbook about it then the book would be a horrible history, wouldn't it?

And guess what? You're about to read it.

It's full of sad and savage stories and sickly spells. But DON'T try them at home! They won't work. They're only there to show what curious creatures we can be at times.

Remember, no one with half a brain believes in witches today...

Witches twisted timeline

T he word 'witch' may come from the old English word 'wicce' which means 'wise person'.

PLEASE, SIR, I THINK YOU'RE A 'WISE PERSON'

X=Y(0. Y-X

THANK YOU GARY!

HEH! HEH!

Other people say it is from the word 'wik' which means 'twisted'. All we need to know is it now means a person who meddles in magic. And witches have been around a long, long time.

AD 100 A Roman writer called Octavius writes about witches that he's heard of. He says…

I am told that they worship the head of a donkey. They have sacrifices where a young priest stabs a baby to death. Then – it's horrible! – they hungrily drink the child's blood, and struggle with one another as they divide his arms and legs.

GULP!

AD 415 In Alexandria (Egypt) the Greek woman Hypatia is murdered by the Christians. They take her to their church, strip her, and then kill her with broken tiles. They call her a witch – her crime is she is into maths! Her corpse is burned.

WHAT DO YOU GET IF YOU ADD TWO AND THREE, GARY?

FIRE!

AD 785 Emperor Charlemagne says there are no such things as witches. Anyone who burns a witch will be executed.

AD 990 Aelfric is an English monk from Winchester. He writes…

Witches meet at crossroads after a funeral. They call to the devil and he appears in the shape of the dead man.

He believes crossroads are the places where spirits of the dead hang around. The witches can have a chat. How would the spirits feel about being dragged from their grave to that place? Dead cross.

1231 Conrad of Marburg is the first witchfinder in Germany. He says…

> *We would gladly burn a hundred if just one of them was guilty.*

1280 First pictures appear in art of witches flying on brooms.

1324 Petronella is the first person to be burnt as a witch in the British Isles.

1390 First 'witch-hunt' in France. A witch was a criminal in the eyes of the Church, but the Church couldn't execute anyone. They handed them over to the court to do the witch killing.

1431 The English capture French warrior Joan of Arc and accuse her of witchcraft. She is burned alive.

1542 Henry VIII introduced a law that says anyone calling up an evil spirit from Hell will die … and all their wealth will go to the king. The law wanted to stop four wicked witch things…

1. 'Fortune-telling' – no one could say, 'The king is going to die!' and start a panic in England.

2. 'Killing someone by making a picture of an enemy and destroying it' – the enemy would die, they said.

3. 'Making a witch's brew so someone would fall in love with you' – a love 'potion'.

4. Making a model of another person. If you were caught you'd be executed AND King Henry would take everything you owned.

The law was used for six years. But … only ONE man was ever arrested. And he was set free!

1547 New king, Edward VI, scraps Henry's law. But…

1563 Queen Elizabeth I says calling up evil spirits gets you a year in jail. Do it a second time and you'll be executed.

1597 James VI of Scotland writes a book about witchcraft, called *Demonology*. He says…

> *The Devil teaches witches how to make pictures of their enemies in wax or clay. Then, by roasting the pictures, their enemies melt or die away by sickness.*

1609 Savage Bamberg trials start in Germany. The witchfinder is Bishop Gottfried von Dornheim. This man of God gets all the wealth of the victims once they are dead! Of course, he has hundreds executed.

1645 In England, witchfinder-general Matthew Hopkins leads the Chelmsford witch trials. Hundreds of witches hang because of this stupid man.

1684 In England, the last woman to hang for witchcraft is Alice Molland.

1692 America goes wild about witches. In Salem, dozens of lucky people are thrown into jail. Nineteen unlucky ones are hanged. One really unlucky farmer is crushed to death under stones and takes two days to die. He is 80 years old.

1712 Jane Wenham is found guilty of witchcraft in Hertfordshire – the last woman to be sentenced to death as a witch in England. In fact, Queen Anne lets her off[1].

1727 In Scotland the last woman to burn as a witch is Janet Horne. But hundreds of years later people still believe in witches…

1 Ann Thorn accused Jane of turning into a cat … but later said she was in a bad mood because her boyfriend dumped her. Jane lives on to 88.

1875 In Long Compton, near Wychwood Forest, the body of an old woman is discovered. Ann Turner had been pinned to the ground by a pitchfork. James Heywood, a local farmer, had once said…

It's she who brings the floods and drought. Her spells withered the crops in the field. Her curse drove my father to an early grave!

Heywood went to prison for her murder.

1928 A family of Hungarian peasants beat an old woman to death because they think she is a witch. They go free.

1945 Charles Walton, a farm worker, is found near Long Compton (again) pinned to the ground by a pitchfork (again). Local gossip says he was a witch. His killer is never caught.

how to spot a witch

People believed that witches were ugly or had odd bodies. This is nonsense of course[2].

There have been many ways that witches have been spotted in the past...

• **Extra fingers** – Queen Anne Boleyn (wife of Henry VIII) was said to be a witch because she had six fingers on one hand. But the people who said that hadn't actually seen her. She could have had ten fingers…

• **Having a lump on the neck** – again Anne Boleyn had this. The lump didn't stop the sword slicing through her neck when she was beheaded, though!

THE LUMP'S GOING TO COST EXTRA

•**Whiffy witches** – an Italian monk called Ludovico Sinistrari said…

YOU CAN SPOT A WITCH BY THEIR SMELL! A WITCH PONGS TERRIBLY!

2 In fact some of my best friends are ugly. Well, to be honest ALL of my friends are ugly. I only knock around with them because they are so ugly they make me look good!

Ludovico lived in the late 1600s. He could even tell you WHY witches smelled! He explained…

EVERY WITCH HAS A 'FAMILIAR' – A SPIRIT SENT FROM THE DEVIL

YOU CANNOT SEE A SPIRIT SO THE DEVIL PUTS THE SPIRIT INTO A CORPSE

THE CORPSE STINKS AND THE STINK HANGS AROUND THE WITCH!

IT'S A DEAD-END JOB!

• **Cauldron** – a witch's cooking pot. William Lord Soulis was said to be a witch in Scotland in the 1300s. He was executed by being boiled in his own cauldron.

IT'S A SOUP-ER WAY TO GO!

I KNEW MY MAGIC WOULD GET ME INTO HOT WATER!

- **Broomsticks** – women who went to a meeting of witches (a 'coven') were supposed to take a broom with them. They then rode the broom like a hobby horse, pretending to be knights riding into the court of their king.

The brush end of the broom went first (like the mane of the horse) and the stick trailed on the ground.

HORRIBLE HISTORIES NOTE

If you see a picture of a witch riding with the brush behind them then either **(a)** the artist is a dummy or **(b)** the witch is flying backwards.

Terrible tests

There were lots of ways to 'test' a suspected witch and the tests were really terrible...

1. Swimming

Witches were tested with the famous 'swimming' trial. To do it properly:

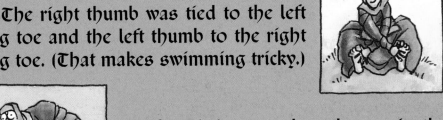

• The right thumb was tied to the left big toe and the left thumb to the right big toe. (That makes swimming tricky.)

• The victim was then thrown in the water.

• If they floated the Devil was helping them – they were taken out and executed.

• If they sank they were innocent – probably dead innocent.

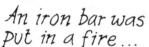

❧ DID YOU KNOW...? ❧

A woman who nagged her husband was known as a 'scold'. Her punishment was to be tied to a stool and dumped in a cold river. This would be done over and over again to teach her a lesson and was called 'ducking'. Some people mix this up with the 'swimming' test but *Horrible Histories* readers know better, don't you?

Ducking went on until 1817 when Sarah Leeke was ducked. It all ended as a bit of a joke as they couldn't get Sarah under the water. The pool they'd chosen was too shallow!

2. Trial by ordeal

The Saxons believed in 'trial by ordeal' – if you could pass a painful test you could go free. Even after the Normans ruled the country (after 1066) a Saxon could choose this kind of trial. In 1209 Agnes, wife of Odo, chose to have a 'trial by ordeal'. She was the first woman to be tried as a witch in England.

An iron bar was put in a fire...

Alice gripped the hot bar in her hand...

She walked nine steps with the bar in her hand

Her hand was bandaged and left...

The bandages were then taken off...

Her hand was healed so she was innocent

3. Eating jam and bread

The Irish believed witches took the form of humans but could not eat human food. Michael Cleary tested his witch-wife by forcing her to eat jam and bread. She ate it ... but he killed her anyway.

4. Staying calm

In 1595 Judt van Dorren was tried as a witch in the village of Mierlo, in the Netherlands. She was tested with ducking and failed. She was arrested. A writer at the time said...

When she was arrested and thrown in prison she was never seen to cry or to look miserable. A normal woman would. She must be guilty.

The writer went on to say that Judt 'looked' guilty so of course she was! Poor Judt was burned.

5. Screaming fits

Some people said they screamed as soon as a witch touched them. In Suffolk in 1664 Rose Cullender said she screamed when witch Amy Duny touched her.

So a law officer tested her.

ROSE CULLENDER FACED AMY DUNY...

I'LL SCREAM IF SHE TOUCHES ME!

AN APRON WAS PLACED IN FRONT OF ROSE'S FACE...

THE OFFICER TOUCHED ROSE...

AIEEE! SHE TOUCHED ME!

THE OFFICER TOLD THE JUDGE

ROSE CULLENDER IS A FAKE

AMY DUNY WILL HANG ANYWAY

She did.

6. Bleeding corpses

Christina Wilson was executed as a witch in Dalkeith, Scotland in 1551. She was said to have killed a man by witchcraft.

She was led to the corpse of her victim. When she touched the corpse, it began to bleed. They said that proved she was the killer and that she was a witch.

7. Prick that witch

People believed a witch was touched by the Devil. On the spot he touched her she would not bleed. So, witchfinders searched witches for the spot and pricked it. If it didn't bleed then the witch could be executed.

John Kincaid of Dalkeith in Scotland was a witch-pricker. He was paid £6 to test a witch. He said Janet Peaston was a witch...

I passed her house and heard her talking to herself. Only witches talk to themselves!

Janet Peaston was 'pricked' by Kincaid. He said she didn't bleed ... but he could have cheated.

Janet was burned. Kincaid was £6 richer.

8. Turcas

This cheerful little toy was used to tear out witches' fingernails if they refused to confess.

☠ DID YOU KNOW...? ☠

If anyone could not be PROVED to be a witch they would still be branded on the cheek and banned from the city. You lost witch-ever way the trial went.

Witch words

There have been lots of wise words for witches through the ages. Here are some useful ones to know...

1. Abracadabra

A piece of word-magic in the Middle Ages was the word Abracadabra. This was said to be a Hebrew charm made from the initials of the Father, the Son and the Holy Spirit. The word was written on paper and hung from the neck by a linen thread for luck.

If you want to try it then it must be written like this...

2. Hocus pocus

Want to turn your deadliest enemy into a frog? Or, worse, a prince? Or, worst of all, a teacher? Then you need magical wicked words like 'hocus pocus'.

There are two stories about how hocus pocus came to be used by magicians.

IT COMES FROM THE NAME OF AN OLD NORSE GOD, OCHUS BOCUS

IT COMES FROM THE ROMAN CATHOLIC CHURCH SERVICE. IT IS A SHORT FORM OF HOC EST CORPUS MEUM – 'THIS IS MY BODY'

3. Pyrzqxgl

Tired of your ugly body? Want a change? Or tired of teacher's ugly mush and want to be taught by someone with film-star looks? Say the word 'Pyrzqxgl' and your wish will come true.

Just two small catches…

a) You have to pronounce it properly.

b) This was invented by L. Frank Baum and used in his book *The Magic of Oz*. So don't get too excited, you will probably be disappointed.

4. Athame

This is a witch's special knife. It is usually double bladed with a black handle and made of steel.

THUD!

5. Venefica

A witch from Italy who poisons people using magical potions.

In the 1600s, Teofania di Adamo invented a poison called 'Aqua Tofana'. Two hundred years later, the famous composer Mozart was supposed to have been poisoned by Aqua Tofana.

6. Agla

Got a poltergeist in the pantry or a spook in the spare room? Get rid of it with the word 'Agla'. This is a short way of saying the Hebrew words that mean 'Thou art forever mighty, Lord'.

7. Cheerful charms – Ananisapta

Got a spot on your nose? Magic it away with 'ananisapta'.

No, it's not a new type of antiseptic cream. It's the magic word. Write it on a parchment and wear it round your neck. (If you don't get better within a week then see your doctor.)

8. Cheerful charms – Hola Nola Massa

Hola Nola Massa was a magic spell from the Middle Ages. It was used to protect you from evils (like homework, housework or boys who pick their noses).

Recite this charm…

(You might like to stand on one leg and wave your arms like aeroplane propellers while you chant this. It won't make the spell work any better but it will make sure those boys who pick their noses keep well away from you.)

**HORRIBLE HISTORIES
HOPELESS JOKE:**

Why do witches wear name badges?
So they can tell which witch is which!

Witch end

Not all witches were executed, but many victims of witch trials came to nasty ends. So nasty you wouldn't want to read about them. You would? Oh, very well ... you asked for it.

Petronella's pain

A serving girl called Petronella was the first person to be burnt as a witch in the British Isles.

Her mistress, Lady Alice Kytler, lived in Kilkenny, Ireland. Three husbands had died and left her rich. Her fourth husband searched her rooms and found magical materials.

Alice was arrested for witchcraft. It was said she made a magical poison that killed her husbands…

Hubby's bump-off brews

you need:

The skull of a robber who's been beheaded.
The nails from a dead man's hand. A baby's brains.
Hair. Worms. Guts. Poison herbs.

To make:

Mash the ingredient in the dead robber's skull and boil it.[3] Leave to cool.

Feed to the husband you want rid of.

3 No, I don't understand how you can boil something in a dead man's head. They never taught me that in skull … I mean school.

Alice was sent to trial along with her son, William Outlawe, and her servant Petronella.

Alice was rich and bribed the judges to let her escape to England.

William was rich and paid for a new lead roof on the cathedral. He was set free.

But Petronella was poor. She was whipped till she confessed she was a witch. Then, on 3 November 1324, she was taken into the city centre and burned alive.

☠ DID YOU KNOW...? ☠

William's new lead covering on Kilkenny cathedral didn't last long. It was so heavy it dragged the roof down and sent the bell tower crashing too. Several people were killed. Bad luck? Or poor Petronella's revenge?

The witch of Irongray

Here is the story of a horrible end for an old woman in Scotland...

In the reign of James I (1603–25), or in the early years of his son Charles's reign (1625–49), a woman was burned as a witch in the parish of Irongray in Scotland. She lived in a little mud-walled cottage and earned a little money by spinning wool and

weaving stockings. She lived alone and was often seen on a summer's evening sitting on a jagged rock above the Routing Stream. Sometimes, late in the evening, she would gather sticks from among the rowan tree roots. She kept a black letter Bible lying in her window which had two brass clasps of a grotesque design to fasten it closed. When she went to church her lips were sometimes seen to be moving. She was known to forecast showers or sunshine at certain times — and her forecasts were often right.

The Bishop of Galloway was urged to punish this witch. He was afraid he'd be reported to the king if he failed to deal with her, so he ordered her to be brought before him near to the Routing Stream. She was dragged roughly from her home. Several neighbours were called to declare the wicked things that she had done.

She was sentenced to be drowned in the Routing Stream. But the crowd insisted that she should be shut up in a tar barrel and thrown into the River Cluden. Unwillingly, the bishop agreed. The wretched woman was enclosed in a barrel, which was set fire to and rolled in a blaze into the waters of the Cluden.

Witch away with it

Some witches got away with their so-called crimes.

Eleanor and the candle

In 1441 Eleanor Cobham wanted her hubby Humphrey to be king. Humphrey's brother, John, was one of the people who stood in the way.

John died.

A man called Hume stepped forward…

Hume went free.

Thomas died in prison.

Roger was hanged.

Margery was burned alive.

And Eleanor? She was forced to walk through the streets of London, carrying a candle.

Did she escape with her life because she was a duchess? Was Margery burned because she was a common villager?

Punishments for witches varied (see pages 50–56), but Margery wasn't punished for being a witch – she was punished for plotting against the life of the king … 'treason'. The punishment for women who committed treason in England was to be burned alive.

White witch powder

Around 1650, in northern England, a poor man suddenly became quite rich. He sold a white powder that cured sick people. He was arrested and asked, 'Did the powder come from evil spirits?'

Now YOU would say, 'Of course not!' But this man told a fantasy story about meeting a tribe of fairy spirits. He said…

SHE TOOK ME TO A HILL, KNOCKED THREE TIMES AND THE HILL OPENED UP

A CAVE!

INSIDE I SAW A QUEEN ON HER THRONE WITH A CROWD OF FAIRY SPIRITS...

TAKE THIS WHITE POWDER- IT IS GOOD MAGIC AND WILL CURE SICK PEOPLE

I'LL DO GOOD AND FEED MY FAMILY

EVERY TIME I NEED MORE POWDER I GO TO THE HILL AND KNOCK THREE TIMES

WELCOME FRIEND

I HAVE CURED MANY PEOPLE AND DONE NO HARM

WHAT A FAIRY STORY

The judge thought the story was a lot of nonsense. He said the man should be whipped all the way to his fairy hill till he saw a bit of sense.

Of course, the court COULD have had him hanged for talking to spirits – it was a sign of witchcraft.

But the people of the village said, 'Not guilty' – and the man went free.

He lived on, rich and happy.

Clarke Clear

The last serious witch charge in England was in 1717. Jane Clarke, from Leicester, was accused of being a witch. A lot of people wanted to go to court and say she was a witch. But the law officers threw out the case.

Janet Horne in Scotland wasn't so lucky ten years later. She was burned in a barrel of tar.

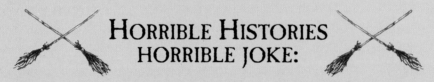

HORRIBLE HISTORIES
HORRIBLE JOKE:

What is a witch's favourite computer program?
Her spell-checker.

Witch I am

Throughout history, so many people have believed in witches they could have made front-page news ... if there had been newspapers. Here are ten true stories as they MIGHT have appeared. But some witch-hunter has snipped the key words.

These are the missing words ... but in the wrong order: broomstick, soldier, coffin, nunnery, head of a corpse, horse, rope, chicken, flea, husband.

Put the right words in the right place. Make sure you SPELL them correctly. Spell ... witches, joke, geddit? Oh, never mind.

1. Yesterday a witch was set free after he promised never to do it again. His spell-book, skull and _____ were burned in the town square. (England, 1307)

2. Bessie Dunlop was burned today for witchcraft. She was known as the Witch of Dalry. She said she was helped by a _____ called Thomas Reid. But Reid died 30 years ago! (Scotland, 1576)

3. King Henry VIII passed a new law today. The law says you are not allowed to make a model of a man, woman or child. Nor can you make a model of an angel, a devil or a _____. (English law, 1542)

4. Elizabeth Francis of Essex said she used witchcraft to make her _____ lame. She was sent to prison for a year. (England, 1566)

5. Anne Armstrong of Corbridge said she changed herself into a _____ so her friend Jane Baites could ride on her back. (England, 1673)

6. Isobel Gowdie slipped off to witch meetings at night, but her husband didn't know she was gone. She slipped a ____ into her place in bed. (Scotland, 1662)

7. A South African woman was said to have flown by riding on the back of a _____. (South Africa, 1800s)

8. Urbain Grandier was burned alive because he sent devils to attack a _____. (France, 1630)

9. Edmund Hartley made a magic circle and was hanged twice because the _____ broke the first time. (England, 1596)

10. A girl in Salem poured an egg white into a glass of water and saw a sign of the future – it was her _____. (America, 1692)

Wild witch-hunts

There were times when people went potty and started to see witches everywhere. They panicked. They really believed their friends and neighbours were witches. Great witch-hunts started and thousands died.

Terrible torture

If a witch said, 'I'm a witch!' they were burned. If a witch said, 'I'm not a witch!' they were tortured till they admitted they WERE a witch.

That's what happened to the Pappenheimer family in the early 1500s in Bavaria, Germany. This husband, wife and three sons made a living by cleaning out toilet pits.

Duke Maximilian I of Bavaria wanted the family to have a 'show' trial. This trial would show everyone in his country that 'crime does not pay'.

When they refused to confess they were tortured. They suffered…

THE STRAPPADO… THE VICTIMS' HANDS WERE TIED BEHIND THEIR BACKS. A ROPE ROUND THEIR WRISTS AND OVER A BEAM HOISTED THEM UP.

THE VICTIMS WERE LIFTED AND DROPPED TIME AFTER TIME.

IF THAT DIDN'T WORK THEY SUFFERED 'SQUASSATION', WHERE WEIGHTS WERE FASTENED TO THEIR FEET AS THEY HUNG THERE.

MANY TORTURERS PUT ON THUMBSCREWS WHILE THE VICTIMS WERE ON THE STRAPPADO.

Four squassations usually led to death.

After long torture, the Pappenheimers said they'd done a ridiculous amount of crimes. Almost every unsolved Bavarian crime of the last ten years.

Over 400 other people were named by the Pappenheimers – many of the people did not exist.

- They were taken to the market place and tied to stakes.
- Their flesh was nipped off with red-hot pincers.
- They were given wine and driven off in carts to their executions.
- They were tied to a wooden frame.
- A heavy wheel was dropped on their limbs to smash them one at a time.
- They were tied to chairs, placed on a bonfire and burned alive.
- The youngest son, Hansel, was forced to watch every minute of his parents' agony.
- After the execution, Hansel was taken back to his cell.
- On 26 November 1600, he was burned to death at the stake.

Witch's woe

There were terrible witch-hunts in Germany in the 1620s. One victim at Bamberg was Johannes Junius. Before he was taken from prison to be burned, he managed to write a letter to his daughter Veronica…

A hundred thousand good-nights, dearly loved daughter Veronica. Innocent have I came into prison, innocent I have been tortured, innocent, now must I die…

…for whoever comes into the witch prison must become a witch or be tortured until he invents something out of his head. The executioner put the thumbscrews on me so that the blood spurted from the nails and everywhere. For four weeks I could not use my hands.

Then they stripped me, bound my hands behind me and tied the rope to a beam. They sent me up on the ladder then took it away. Eight times did they draw me up and let me fall again, so that I suffered terrible agony.

With God's help I took the torture. At last the executioner led me back into the cell and he spoke to me: Sir, I beg you, for God's sake, confess something, whether it be true or not. Invent something. Even if you bear the torture you will not escape, not even if you were an earl. One torture will follow another until you say you are a witch.

Dear child, keep this letter secret, so that people do not find it, or I shall be tortured most cruelly and the jailers will be beheaded. Dear child, pay the messenger a thaler[4]… I have taken several days to write this – my hands are both crippled. I am in a sad state. Good night, for your father Johannes Junius will never see you again.

4 A thaler was a silver coin in the Middle Ages.

In the end Johannes Junius did confess to being a witch, and in August 1628 he was burned at the stake.

Bamberg babes

There were hundreds of German witch trials at Bamberg in the 1620s.

Victims were tortured with...

MY DUCK'S MELTED!

Boiling baths.

I THINK I'VE DISCOVERED HOT-PANTS!

Roasting on a hot iron chair.

THIS IS DEFINITELY A LOW POINT!

Kneeling on spikes.

On their way to execution the victims had their hands cut off. Children as young as six months were tortured and executed.

The Salem witches

It all started in Salem, Massachusetts, in 1692, when three little girls aged nine, ten and twelve became the cause of death and trouble. When Betty, Abigail and Ann started acting strangely, the doctor came up with the answer...

> THEY HAVE BEEN TOUCHED BY THE EVIL HAND! THEY ARE BEWITCHED!

Who could they blame? Betty's dad was the minister – so you couldn't blame him! But the family had a black slave, Tituba, who had been teaching the girls how to tell fortunes. It would be easy to blame her!

Now, the witch-hunting rules were simple:

> CONFESS AND YOUR LIFE WILL BE SPARED!

> I CONFESS! SPARE ME!

> NOT YET! YOU MUST TELL US THE NAMES OF OTHER WITCHES IN SALEM – OR WE'LL EXECUTE YOU!

> OH, IN THAT CASE...THEIR NAMES ARE...

Of course, everyone accused had to accuse someone else to save their life and so it went on. A hundred and fifty people were accused of being witches – even though they knew they weren't!

They said daft things like…

YES, I FLEW ON A BROOMSTICK AND MARRIED THE DEVIL!

Then Betty, Abigail and Ann said…

WE MADE IT ALL UP FOR SPORT!

That should have put a stop to it. But the accusers said…

NO! THESE WITCHES HAVE ADMITTED THEY ARE WITCHES

So nineteen women were hanged. But the worst fate was saved for one of the men. He refused to say if he was guilty or not guilty. His punishment was to have stones piled on top of him till he suffocated and was crushed to death.

All because three little liars had some 'sport'.

KIDS, EH!

Cruel kids

In the 1500s and 1600s, everyone was mixed up in witch-hunting. Children too...

Evil Edmund

Village wise women made a little money by telling fortunes, making simple cures for sick animals and people, or finding something a villager had lost.

The problem was, the wise woman could be called a 'witch' for doing these things. If you upset someone they could report you and put your life in danger. Even if you DIDN'T upset them they could report you for another reason.

That's what happened in the village of Fence in Lancashire at Halloween, 1632.

Edmund's father later told the truth about his son...

Our Edmund isn't a bad lad. A bit imaginative. But not BAD.

He told a story about being out on the moors near Fence ... that's the village of Fence. And he saw two greyhounds trailing chains.

He said he wanted the hounds to hunt a hare but when they refused to run he beat them with a stick ... and that made them turn into humans!

He knew the woman responsible at once. It was Frances Dickenson, our next door neighbour.

He said she promised him money if he kept quiet. He refused of course. He knew witchcraft when he saw it.

So they tied him up. Then Frances turned her friend into a white horse and stuck our little Edmund on its back. They took him to a witches' coven, where he saw witches and warlocks feasting. Naturally he thought he was going to be a sacrifice ... well, you would.

But he ran away and told the magistrate. Old Frances Dickenson was arrested and charged ... Along with a lot of other people. They were all sentenced to death. All on the word of our Edmund.

But the judge delayed the executions. Just as well as it turned out.

Our Ed was quite a celebrity! Claimed to be able to hunt down witches by sight. He was paid for every one he pointed out. He made a lot of money.

A lot.

Then he was shown to be a liar. The witches were set free and they looked into Edmund's story. It seems he was put up to it.

Who put him up to it?

It was me. We made a lot of money. A lot.

It wasn't just Edmund's dad who made money from Frances Dickenson's misery. A writer turned the witch story into a play called *The Late Lancashire Witches*. It was popular in London.

A vicar called John Webster met Edmund and wrote a book about his witch-spotting trick. Everyone made money from the story … except the poor men and women who were locked away for months in Lancaster's chilly castle.

Bad boys
Lots of boys told lies about witches. In England in the 1600s these included…

'The Leicester Boy'
John Smith was a four-year-old fraud … no one was executed. But in 1616 when he was thirteen he tried again. This time his lies had nine women executed and one died in jail.

'The Burton Boy'
Alice Goodrich was accused of being a witch by a boy called Thomas Darling. He made up the story. But innocent Alice died in prison at Derby while she was waiting to go on trial.

'The Bilson Boy'
In 1620 William Perry said witches tortured him … then he said he only lied because he liked people to take notice of him. A priest taught him to fake his torment by 'vomiting rags, thread, straw and crooked pins'.

BLAH!

Gruesome girls
But girls could often beat the boys when it came to lies…

The Bargarran Impostor
The lies of an eleven-year-old girl named Christine Shaw led to 21 people being accused. Seven of them burned at the stake in Paisley. Christine suffered from fits and cried out that certain people were torturing her with their spirits. This trial was also known as 'The Renfrewshire Witches'.

Siri Jorgensdatter
A thirteen-year-old Norwegian girl told law officers that her grandmother was a witch who took her to the Blakulla feast with the Devil.

Anne Durant of Bury St Edmunds
Anne said a local witch sent ghosts to scare her in 1660. The witch was hanged.

Witch cures

In the Middle Ages there were very few doctors. If you were rich you could afford to pay for a doctor, but poor villagers had to make do with a 'wise' man or woman.

You could ask a wise person to find something you'd lost. You could ask them to look into the future. These people had some real cures that used herbs, and some magical ones. These wise people were often called witches.

Which witch cures would work?

HORRIBLE HISTORIES NOTE

The readers of this book are warned NOT to try any of these cures at home. Even if they don't kill you they could make you ill. Read them for fun and nothing else.

Warts

There are dozens of cures for warts. You could try rubbing the wart on a pig's back, for example.

OR YOU COULD TRY THE CHEMIST!

Baby rash

Give your baby's rash a bash with this cute cure from the Middle Ages...

> Take a lock of woman's hair
> Burn it in the open air.
> Snakes and serpents won't come near
> For the smoke they truly fear.
>
> Rub the burnt hair in sore eyes,
> Or on warts, and they will fly.
> Mix some honey with the ash,
> It will cure a baby's rash.

Headache

Go along to a public hanging. When the criminal is dead and has been cut down, buy a piece of the rope from the hangman. Rub the rope against your head and the headache will go.

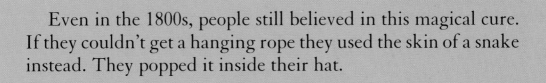

WELL, IT WORKED FOR THE CRIMINAL, DIDN'T IT? HE WON'T BE HAVING ANY MORE HEADACHES!

Even in the 1800s, people still believed in this magical cure. If they couldn't get a hanging rope they used the skin of a snake instead. They popped it inside their hat.

Earache
Mix together…

Mix these and put them in the sore ear. Then take some black wool and use it as an earplug. After all, you wouldn't want the cockroach to escape, would you?

The Bedale Book of Witchcraft (1773) says you should use frog's spit. But the book doesn't tell us how you get the frog to spit.

Are frogs like humans? Is it only the rude ones that spit?

Spell-ing test
Here are eight magic spells and what they do – but they are scrambled. Can you sort them out?

The prize for getting them right is being burned as a witch – well, you'd have to be a witch to know the answers!

The prize for getting any wrong is being turned into a frog – unless you are a frog, in which case the prize is being turned into a horrible historian.

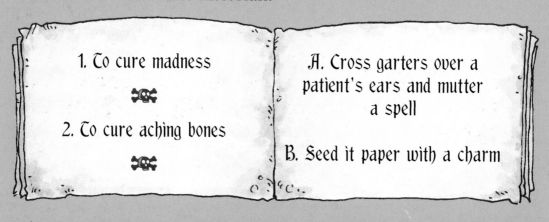

1. To cure madness

2. To cure aching bones

A. Cross garters over a patient's ears and mutter a spell

B. Seed it paper with a charm

3. To make someone fall in love with you

✖

4. To cure a mad dog

✖

5. To cure a headache

✖

6. To cure animal sickness

✖

7. To cure heartache

✖

8. To find the name of a criminal

C. Jump in a river.

D. Release a live bat in the room of the sufferer

E. Scatter rose petals in their path

F. Write the names of suspects on pieces of paper and place them one at a time inside a Bible

G. Boil some of the sufferer's hair in their urine then throw it on a fire

H. Tie herbs to the animal's tail or tap them with a magic wand

Answers: 1) D, 2) C, 3) E, 4) B, 5) G, 6) H, 7) A, 8) F Note: 8) F – The Bible will shake when the guilty name is put in.

How did you do?

I SCORED TEN! AM I A WITCH?

NO, YOU'RE A CHEAT! THERE ARE ONLY EIGHT

Witch law
is witch?

You aren't daft enough to believe in witchcraft. But the clever people who make the law are! Here are some of the weirdly witchy punishments witches have been whacked with.

5: PILLORY
DON'T EVEN THINK ABOUT IT!
6: HEAD SCROLL
WHAT A DUNCE!
7: BEHEADING
IF ONE MORE PERSON SAYS 'JUST A LITTLE OFF THE TOP PLEASE', I'LL SCREAM!
8: STONING
10: GOUGING
THIS IS POTTY
9: BURNING

Here's how the putrid punishments worked...

1. Forced fasting

Around AD 670, the Archbishop of Canterbury said the punishment for being a witch was to go hungry...

2. Exile

In the AD 860s, King Aethelred decided it was better to get rid of witches from his kingdom – witches made Aethel see red...

But less than a hundred years later, King Aethelstan decided witches should be killed. This Aethel couldn't *stan* the sight of them.

3. Hanging

In 1563, a law was passed that said witches in England and Scotland must die. English witches were hanged, Scottish witches were burned.

In 1566 Agnes Waterhouse was found guilty, and hanged at Chelmsford. Her crime?

YOU HAVE BEEN FOUND GUILTY OF USING YOUR CAT CALLED SATAN, TO KILL A MAN WHO UPSET YOU. SATAN ALSO DESTROYED LOCAL CATTLE, SPOILED A NEIGHBOUR'S BUTTER, KILLED ANOTHER NEIGHBOUR'S GOOSE AND MURDERED YOUR OWN HUSBAND AS WELL. I SENTENCE YOU TO HANG BY THE NECK UNTIL YOU ARE DEAD

AND MAY GOD HAVE MERCY ON YOUR SOUL

PURR-FECT!

4. Drowning

In the AD 990s, the King of Norway, Olaf Tryggvason, orders that male witches are tied up and left on a small rocky island. When the tide came in they drowned.

5. Pillory

John Berking, a London fortune-teller, was arrested in 1390. His crime was telling people their future. Berking spent one hour in the pillory, two weeks in jail, and he was banished from London.

6. Head scroll

In 1467, William Byg from South Yorkshire was arrested for looking into a crystal ball. He said the glass ball would tell him the names of some thieves. Byg was forced to appear in public with a scroll on his head. This scroll said he was a fortune-teller.

For hundreds of years teachers copied this idea of a sign-on-the-head to show you up!

7. Beheading

In 1540, people were asking, 'How long will fat King Henry VIII live?'

Lord Hungerford tried to find out using witchcraft. He was caught and his punishment was to be beheaded. He was a lord. Common people like you and me would be hanged, but lords had their heads lopped off.

8. Stoning

The first mention of punishing witches comes in the Bible. In Leviticus 20:27 it is written:

> **A** man or woman who is a wizard shall be put to death; they shall be stoned with stones, their blood shall be upon them.

The ordinary people could all join in with the stoning. They had to use small stones, though, so death was slow and painful.

9. Burning

Witches in Scotland and Europe were burned to death. Usually they were strangled first so they didn't suffer a slow death in the fire.

If the executioner felt really cruel, he'd use damp wood so they burned slowly.

At least four big witch-hunts brought terror to Scotland from 1590 until 1680. In Aberdeen in 1597, 23 women and a man were strangled then burned to ashes. Others were so terrified of dying like that they killed themselves in prison.

Never mind. The people of Aberdeen still shared in the revenge. Their corpses were dragged through the streets till they were torn to pieces.

10. Gouging

In AD 415, the wise woman Hypatia of Alexandria (Egypt) was accused of being a witch. A mob of Christians attacked her. They used broken pottery to gouge out her flesh.

This was a punishment invented by the Roman Emperor Constantine for witches.

Constantine said…

*Witches should have their flesh torn
from their bones with iron hooks.*

The Christians didn't have iron hooks so they used broken cups, pots and plates instead.

WHAT A WAY TO GO! CUT BY CROCKERY AND FLESH PEELED BY PLATES — AND POTS![5]

☠ **DID YOU KNOW?** ☠

People sometimes dealt with witches in their own way. In 1867 the people of Sheep Street in Stratford thought old Jane Ward was a witch. A man called John Davies who lived in the street blamed old Jane for making his daughter sick by sending evil spirits down his chimney. The police refused to arrest old Jane so Davies went out and slashed her face. He said…

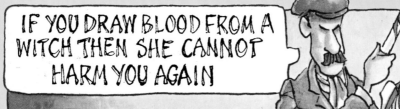

IF YOU DRAW BLOOD FROM A WITCH THEN SHE CANNOT HARM YOU AGAIN

And old Jane never did any more harm to anyone – she died a few days after the attack. Davies went to prison for just six months. Would you believe it? Or (as it happened in Sheep Street) would EWE believe it?

---

5 This is not an easy thing to say when you are alive, never mind when you are being hacked to death, so Hypatia probably said something simpler like, 'Ow! Get that teacup out of my eye!'

Curious curses

We all know someone we dislike. But we don't usually put a curse on them.

If you believed you had witch powers you might try, though. In the horrible past people have tried these curious curses...

1. Drown that king!

In 1591, Agnes Sampson of North Berwick in Scotland was arrested. She was charged with trying to kill King James VI of Scotland by making a storm that would sink his ship.

She said it was true and she told how it was done...

(A) FIRST DIG UP A FRESH CORPSE FROM A GRAVEYARD

(B) CUT OFF ITS ARMS AND LEGS

(C) FASTEN AN ARM OR LEG TO EACH LEG OF A CAT

(D) THROW THE CAT INTO THE SEA WHERE YOU WANT THE STORM PLOP!

James said that Agnes was lying.

I DON'T BELIEVE A WORD YOU SAY

But then Agnes took James to a quiet room. She told him what he had said to his wife on the night they were married. James was shocked.

I BELIEVE EVERY WORD YOU SAY!

Agnes and many of her friends were burned alive.

James went on to become King James I of England and he wrote a book about witchcraft called *Demonology*.

☠ **DID YOU KNOW…?** ☠

When Agnes Sampson wanted to curse King James she tried to get hold of some of his underwear. The plan was to smear it with toad poison and give him burning pain. It didn't work. James never let his knickers out of his sight.

TWO WOMEN HAVE NICKED MY PANTS!

YES, SIR, THEY'RE A PAIR OF NICKERS!

2. The Bathory blood curse

Do you have an enemy you want to get rid of? Want them to die painfully? This curse from 1600s Eastern Europe would have done the trick.

A Spot of Blood

You need:
A black hen, a white stick, your enemy's clothes

To make:
1. Place the black hen on the floor.
2. Use the white stick to batter the hen to death.
3. Keep the blood and smear a drop of it on your enemy.
4. If you cannot get near your enemy take a piece of their clothing and put the blood on that.
5. Your enemy will die in horrible pain like the hen.

Try it today and the GOOD news is you won't go to prison for murder because no one would believe the curse could work.

The BAD news is you would go to prison for cruelty to the hen – and it would serve you right too. Do NOT try this at home.

☠ DID YOU KNOW…? ☠

Elizabeth Bathory (1560–1614), a cruel countess of Transylvania, used this curse. She also tried to get rid of her enemies by having a bath in poison then having the poisonous bath water stirred into a cake that she fed them. They got gut-ache but didn't die.

3. Curse that cow!

Poor French peasants hated the rich farmers. They were jealous of all their money, so some plotted a witchcraft revenge.

In Lorraine, France, in 1597 a woman called Senelle Petter

was charged with cursing a farmer's best animals and making them go lame.

At her trial Senelle told the judge how she did it...

Senelle also cursed a priest – who then died.

4. Kill that enemy!

Witches were said to kill their enemies by making a model of the person they hated. If they wanted to give their enemy a pain in the leg, they stuck a pin in the leg of the model.

If they wanted to KILL the person they stuck a pin in the heart.

How do you make a model of your enemy? In 1566, John Walsh of England explained…

1. TAKE THE SOIL FROM A NEW GRAVE…

2. THEN TAKE THE RIB OF A MAN OR WOMAN BURNED TO ASHES[6]

3. ADD A BLACK SPIDER AND THE SAP FROM AN ELDER TREE

4. HERE'S ONE I MADE EARLIER — IT'S A MODEL OF ME, OF COURSE!

5. STICK A PIN IN THE HEART AND THE VICTIM WILL DIE IN NINE DAYS…

6. …OH DEAR!

In 1586, an Italian magician called Girolamo Menghi said he knew a witch who made a model out of feathers. Was the victim tickled to death?

6 How could you take their rib if they've been burned to ashes? I don't know. If you really MUST know you'll have to ask John Walsh. Good luck.

5. Eat that enemy!

In the Scottish witch-hunts of 1657–61 Isobel Craig of North Berwick was accused of being a witch. She cursed another woman with the words…

The woman scratched Isobel because that is supposed to stop the witch's curse working.

6. Boil that boy!

In 1619, Joan Flower and her daughters were servants at Belvoir Castle in Leicestershire, England. One of the daughters, Margaret, was sacked for pinching stuff. Joan decided to take revenge on the lord's sons.

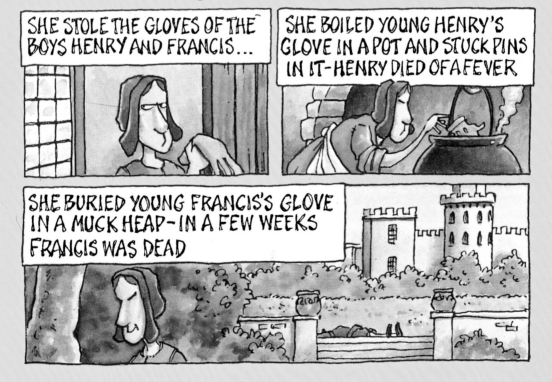

The Flower family was arrested. Joan sneered at the judges…

They gave her bread.
She choked and died on the spot.
Creepy, eh?

7. Charm licking

This was used by many people to break a spell. If you think you are cursed by a witch, then take a lucky charm…

- Lick the charm in an up and down motion.
- Then lick it in an across back and forth motion.
- Then lick it in an up and down motion again.

If you can taste a salty taste on your tongue then you have destroyed the curse.

Witch quiz

How much do you know about witches? Test yourself with this quiz. Score ten and you probably had the Devil to help you ... so you will be sentenced to death! (But it is death by old age so you don't have to worry yet.)

Score 0 and you must be an angel.

1. In the 1500s you could be executed for believing what?
a) That rubbing your body in snot and soot makes you invisible.
b) That there are fairies at the bottom of your garden.
c) That the Devil appears in the form of a teacher.

2. Mary Bateman was a trickster. But in Leeds in 1805 she made people believe she was a witch. How?
a) She flew on a broomstick.
b) She made an elephant disappear.
c) She had a hen that laid eggs with messages on them.

3. Marie Baten was arrested as a witch in Mierlo, the Netherlands, in 1595. What did she ask the law to do to her?
a) Duck her to prove she wasn't a witch.
b) Burn her because she was a witch.
c) Cook her and feed her liver to the poor people of Mierlo.

4. In 1894, in Clonmel, Ireland, Bridget Cleary's husband said she showed signs of being a witch. How?

a) She grew warts on her chin.

b) She grew two inches taller.

c) She grew beautiful overnight.

5. People said Agnes Waterhouse of Chelmsford turned her white cat into a toad in 1565. Why did they say she did that?

a) She wanted mittens from her kitten.

b) She wanted fat from her cat.

c) She wanted toad-in-the-hole for dinner.

6. In 1605, in Oxfordshire, Brian Gunter felt guilty because he had killed his neighbours' son. Instead of saying 'sorry' he got his daughter to accuse them of witchcraft. How did he kill their son?

a) In a fight.

b) In a horse and cart accident.

c) Playing football.

7. In America in 1692, a man called Giles Corey refused to admit he was a witch. What did the law do to try and make him talk?

a) Tickled his feet till he couldn't take any more.

b) Pulled out his fingernails, then his toenails, one by one.

c) Crushed him slowly under heavy weights.

Answers:

1b) In 1576, Bessie Dunlop of Ayrshire was accused of witchcraft. She was probably tortured and said...

> *While I was taking a cow out to a field, I came across an old man with a grey beard wearing a grey coat. He wore a black bonnet on his head, and carried a white wand in his hand. He showed me the way to a place where I met four men and eight women of Elfame[7]. They were dressed as humans but very smartly, the men like gentlemen, and the women had tartan shawls about them. They were very friendly towards me, and asked me to travel with them to Elfame. They told me that in Elfame I would be well fed and beautiful, but I would not go with them.*

She was burned just for believing in the fairies.

2c) People paid a penny to see Mary Bateman's magical hen. When Mary pulled an egg from under the hen it had the words 'Christ is coming' written on it. Of course it was a trick, but a lot of foolish people paid her a lot of money.

Another trick was to 'cure' a Mrs Perigo with a magical pudding. It was full of poison and Mrs Perigo died. Mary Bateman was sentenced to hang.

Even in her death cell she cheated another prisoner out of money. On 20 March 1809, Mary Bateman, the Yorkshire Witch, was led to her execution in front of a large crowd. Some of the Yorkshire people still believed her to have witch powers and that she would somehow escape the noose. She didn't.

7 Elfame – another name for the fairy world.

3a) Marie asked to be ducked. She said…

I WANT TO BE DUCKED THE WAY THEY DID LAST MONTH IN GELDROP. I AM SURE THAT I WILL SINK. ONLY A WITCH WOULD FLOAT!

What happened? They ducked Marie.
What happened next? She floated.
What did they do with her? They burned her alive.
So the poor woman was half-drowned in freezing water AND burned.

4b) Michael Cleary was mentally ill and believed his wife Bridget had been kidnapped. The woman in his house was a fairy who just made herself look like Bridget. Fairies were seen as a sort of witch.

Michael tortured Bridget with the help of friends and family. She was held over the kitchen fire. She screamed…

I AM BRIDGET YOUR WIFE, NOT A FAIRY!

I BELIEVE HER MICHAEL

I DON'T!

Finally, mad Michael poured lamp oil on Bridget and set her on fire. She died horribly.

Michael Cleary went to prison for 20 years – but he always believed it was a fairy he'd burned and not his wife.

5a) Agnes was a widow aged 63. She was arrested for killing William Fyne using witchcraft. At her trial people came up with all sorts of stories about Agnes's 'crimes'. They said she changed her cat Satan into a toad so she could have its warm fur for gloves.

A little girl told an even dafter story. Little Aggie Brown (age twelve) said…

> WIDOW WATERHOUSE HAD A BLACK DOG WITH A FACE LIKE AN APE. IT TRIED TO KILL ME. IT CAME AT ME WITH A DAGGER IN ITS MOUTH AND SAID IT WOULD STICK THE DAGGER IN MY HEART

Aggie never said how the dog could talk with a knife in its mouth or how she got away.

Sensible Mrs Waterhouse said…

> I DON'T EVEN OWN A DAGGER, SILLY CHILD

Then, for some reason, senseless Mrs Waterhouse added…

> MIND YOU, I *DID* LET MY CAT SUCK MY BLOOD THEN I SENT HIM OFF TO KILL MY NEIGHBOUR, WILLIAM FYNE. WELL, I HATED HIM AND USED SATAN TO KILL HIM

Widow Waterhouse was hanged. She was the first woman to be hanged under Elizabeth I's new witchcraft laws.

6c) Brian killed his neighbour's son in a football match. He was breaking up a fight and smashed the poor boy on the head with his knife. (As you know, hitting a player with a knife is a red-card foul today.)

Brian taught his daughter, Anne, to sneeze pins and pretend to have fits. He gave her drugs to make her ill.

When King James visited Oxfordshire, Brian took his case to him. It was thrown out and the three women went free. Brian was locked up for a while.

7c) Giles Corey (one of the Salem witches), refused to say 'Guilty' or 'Not Guilty' when he was charged with witchcraft. (He probably thought they could not go on with the trial. He was wrong.)

Corey was 'pressed'. He was made to lie on the ground with a wooden plank covering him. Heavy boulders were then placed on the plank. The longer he stayed silent the more they put on.

He suffered for two days and then died.

DID YOU KNOW...?

Corey's tongue was forced out of his mouth as the weight pressed on his chest. The sheriff came and forced it back in. Cruel or what?

Wicked witchfinders

Some people said they could tell who was a witch and who wasn't. They said they could look at a group of people and tell which is witch. They couldn't, of course. But they had their own reasons for becoming 'witchfinders'. Usually wicked reasons.

Terrible Tranquille and the nuns of Loudun

In 1630, Father Urbain Grandier, a parish priest in Loudun, France, wrote some very nasty things about Cardinal Richelieu … the most powerful man in France.

Big mistake.

Richelieu heard tales of nuns who were bewitched and they blamed Grandier. Richelieu knew what time it was…

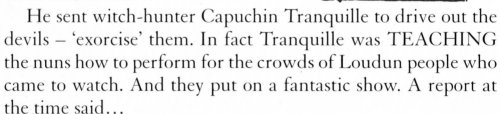

…TIME FOR REVENGE!

He sent witch-hunter Capuchin Tranquille to drive out the devils – 'exorcise' them. In fact Tranquille was TEACHING the nuns how to perform for the crowds of Loudun people who came to watch. And they put on a fantastic show. A report at the time said…

The nuns struck their chests and backs with their heads, as if they had their necks broken. They twisted their arms at the joints of the shoulder, the elbow, or the wrist, two or three times around.

Lying on their stomachs, they joined the palms of their hands to the soles of their feet; their faces became so frightful one could not bear to look at them.

Their eyes remained open without winking. Their tongues shot out from their mouths, horribly swollen, black, hard and covered with pimples.

They threw themselves back till their heads touched their feet, and walked in this position with great speed.

They swore so horribly and so loud that nothing like it was ever heard before.

A crowd of 300 people gathered to see the crazed nuns.

Another enemy of Grandier's, Dr Mannouri, was brought in to test him for the Devil's mark[8].

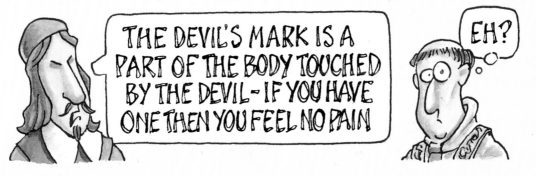

8 Yes, the priest seemed to have a lot of enemies and must have upset a lot of people. A bit like a traffic warden.

Mannouri stuck a round probe into Grandier's body and the priest showed no sign of pain! How could that happen?

Mannouri cheated.

THE PROBE WAS PLACED AGAINST THE VICTIM'S SKIN

THE DOCTOR SEEMED TO PUSH BUT THE HANDLE WENT BACK INTO HIS PALM

Grandier was found guilty, but before he was executed he was tortured. Planks were strapped to his legs. Iron wedges were hammered in between the planks and the legs till the legs were crushed and the marrow and blood spilled out.

Through all the pain Grandier never named another witch. He was taken off and burned.

Some of the nuns said...

SORRY-WE WERE PUT UP TO IT BY TRANQUILLE

THERE'S A SURPRISE! A BIT-OUCH! LATE, MIND YOU-OUCH!

The witchfinder general

Britain's most famous witchfinder was Matthew Hopkins (died 1647) – the witchfinder general. Who gave him that name?

ACTUALLY I GAVE MYSELF THE NAME!

In the 1600s he was the terror of Suffolk, Essex and East Anglia, where he had around 230 people hanged as witches.

Here are six horrible Hopkins facts they never tell you...

1. The prisons became overcrowded with Hopkins victims. In summer the air was so filthy they died of disease. In fact, one report from Colchester in 1645 said...

The air was so foul that dogs, cats, mice and rats died and birds dropped from the sky.

As bad as the boys' toilets in one or two schools!

2. Hopkins thought there were a couple of ways to stop a witch's evil power. They were pretty disgusting so you might like to skip this bit.

YOU CAN BOIL A WITCH'S HAIR IN HER PEE... OR STICK A RED-HOT POKER IN HER POO. THAT WILL DESTROY HER MAGIC

HORRIBLE HISTORIES NOTE
Don't try this in the house as the smell will take days to clear.

3. Elizabeth Clarke of Chelmsford was sentenced to hang after Hopkins had accused her. She was taken to the gallows and told to climb the ladder.

But poor old Elizabeth only had one leg. She had to be helped up the ladder so a noose could be put around her neck.

THEN the ladder was taken away and she was left to die.

4. Crowds rushed forward to grab a piece of a witch's clothes or the rope that hanged her. They wanted to snatch a bit of their magic. So the hangmen took the bodies down as quickly as they could.

Sometimes they took them down TOO quickly. The victim was still alive.

They had to hang them again.

5. The witch was buried in a pit behind the jail. The corpse had a heavy rock placed on top. Sometimes they had a stake of wood driven through them.

This was to stop the witch rising up and going to heaven.

6. Hopkins made sure dozens of men and women hanged for witchcraft. That was the law in England. But ONE poor woman, Mary Lakeland, was burned alive.

Hopkins said she used her witchcraft to murder her husband. And the punishment for killing a husband was to burn. Mary Lakeland was perhaps the only witch to burn in England.

In 1645, in Ipswich she was…

• Dropped into a barrel of tar.

- Chained to a post in the ground (so she couldn't jump out).
- Burned in the tar barrel with a bonfire underneath.

Witchfinder finish

There was a story that Matthew Hopkins was eventually tried as a witch and hanged. It would serve him right.

But that story is probably not true. He most likely died of a lung disease in 1647.

There were no more huge witch-hunts in England. The people found out it cost too much money to pay witchfinders, keep victims in prison and hang them. Hanging a witch cost £1 in the 1640s ... a lot of money ... while burning Mary Lakeland cost over £3.

GOD SAYS, 'YOU SHOULD NOT ALLOW A WITCH TO LIVE'

I KNOW...BUT GOD DOESN'T HAVE TO PAY THE BILLS!

Witchfinders flattened

Being a witch-hunter could be dangerous.

African Zulu chief Shaka (1787–1828) had witchfinders who 'sniffed' witches. He didn't trust them so he set them a test. He said a witch had smeared blood on his house and he wanted the witch found.

Even though Shaka had smeared the blood himself the witchfinders uncovered 300 guilty people!

Shocked Shaka had the witchfinders clubbed to death ... witch serves them right.

Spelling time

Here are a few witch spells. They won't work so don't worry!

1. Hare and back again

Isobel Gowdie was a young housewife. She was tried as a witch in Scotland in 1662. Isobel was happy to talk about her witchy ways. No one tortured her. She just talked herself into trouble.

She shared several of her magic spells with the court. This was what she called out when she wanted to change herself into a hare…

> I shall go into a hare,
> With sorrow and such and much great care;
> And I shall go in the Devil's name,
> Until I come home again.

To change back she would chant:

> Hare, hare, God send thee care.
> I am in a hare's likeness now,
> But I shall be in a woman's likeness even now.

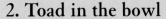

Some historians claim we don't know what happened to her, but some reports say she was strangled and burned.

THAT'S LIFE... HARE TODAY AND GONE TOMORROW

2. Toad in the bowl
Do you live in India and need rain to make your crops grow? Then here's a special spell…

A spell of rain

You need:
A live frog, a wooden bowl used for grinding corn, a corn-crushing stone

To make:
1. Collect water from five homes in the village and put it in the bowl.
2. Take your frog and drop it into the water.
3. The women must sing songs about the drought. If you don't know any then try…

I've got rain on the brain
But I've got none in my drain.
Heavy rain, or just some fog,
Bring rain for my little frog.

4. As you sing, use the crushing stone to grind the frog to a pulp[9].
5. Wait for the rain to start.

9 It is illegal to hurt a frog when there is a 'y' in the name of the day … so it's best to read this spell but not try it.

3. She loves me, she loves me not…
Want to know who you are going to marry?
   Here's how to find out….

① LIGHT A CANDLE AND STAND IN FRONT OF A MIRROR
② PEEL AN APPLE IN FRONT OF THE MIRROR
③ THE FACE OF YOUR FUTURE WIFE OR HUSBAND WILL APPEAR

I THINK I'LL STAY SINGLE THANKS!

☠ DID YOU KNOW…? ☠

If you see a spider on Halloween then it may be the spirit of a dead friend come to watch over you. Ahhhh!

---

4. Spot that spirit
Some people believe there are ghosts all around us. We just can't SEE them. If you really WANT to see them then all you have to do is make an ointment…

To see spirits mix the fat of a lapwing, a bat and a goat.
Rub it into the eyelids.

5. Flying fun

Late for school? Don't worry. Use this medieval witches' spell to fly down the roads and get there on time.

Take a broom out of the cupboard, sit astride it and chant this spell…

**HORSE AND HATTOCK,
HORSE AND GO,
HORSE AND PELATIS, HO, HO!**

Did I mention that this one doesn't work either?

NO!

6. Y ran qui ran

Worried about catching rabies after being bitten by a mad dog? Worry no more. Here is a cure … and you may like to carry it round in your pocket in case you ever come across a mad dog.

DOES IT WORK IF YOU'RE BITTEN BY A MAD TEACHER?

GED-OFF!

Try it … simply write these words on a piece of paper…

Y ran Qui Ran, casram casratem casratosque

Place the paper in an eggshell and force it down the throat of the mad dog's victim.

> HOLD STILL!

> I THINK I'D RATHER BE BITTEN!

☠ DID YOU KNOW…? ☠

There was a strong belief in witchcraft in Africa in the Middle Ages. When Africans were taken to America as slaves some of them took their belief with them. In Haiti the witchcraft became known as Vodun (or 'voodoo'). Writers and film-makers made up a lot of nonsense about Vodun believers.

> THESE VOODOO GUYS KILLED PEOPLE AND DRANK THEIR BLOOD

The truth is all they killed were chickens, goats, sheep and dogs. They believed this brought them good health, good crops or good luck.

> IT WASN'T SO LUCKY FOR THE DEAD DOGS AND CHOPPED CHICKENS!

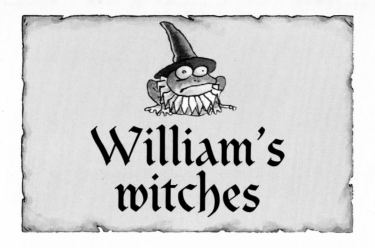

William's witches

By the time James I became King of England and Scotland he had become very interested in witches. The great writer William Shakespeare wrote a 'witch' play to amuse James.

The weird sisters

Shakespeare wrote the play *Macbeth* where the hero, Lord Macbeth, meets three 'weird sisters' who look into the future.

They tell Lord Macbeth he'll be king. And he is ... after he's murdered his way to the top.

Their famous spell is NOT 'hubble bubble, toil and trouble' as many people think. They chant ...

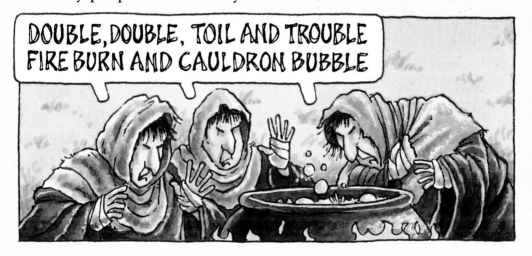

You knew that because you are clever and listened to your Shakespeare in school.

They then threw disgusting things in their pot.

So, clever student, which TWO of this list did Macbeth's witches NOT throw in their pot?

A THE GUTS OF A TIGER

J THE TONGUE OF AN ADDER

D THE WOOL OF A BAT

I THE EYE OF A NEWT

F THE WING OF A BABY OWL

G THE NOSE OF A DEAD BABY

E THE BLOOD OF A BABOON

Wild wizards

Want to make a good fortune? Don't gamble on the lottery. Just visit a wizard and see if he can make you some gold. Of course it would all be a trick and you horrible historians would **NOT** be daft enough to fall for it...

Golden dream

The great dream of medieval magicians was to turn ordinary metal into gold.

About 1450, Bernard of Treviso tried mixing 2,000 eggs with olive oil and sulphuric acid. He cooked it for a fortnight, added metal, and produced ... the world's biggest omelette! It was a failure. He fed it to his pigs. It was probably the best meal they'd ever had.

Just as well, really, since it was the  last meal they ever had.

THAT'S SOW SAD

It poisoned them.

Fool's gold

German wizard David Beuther of Germany knew the secret of making gold (he said). He was tortured to make him tell. How did he keep his secret?

a) He put it in a bottle and threw it in the sea.
b) He wrote it down and swallowed it.
c) He never wrote it down and poisoned himself.

Answer: c) David Beuther was thrown in prison but refused
to tell. When he was set free he poisoned himself.

Maybe Beuther's gold-making was a trick. Here's how to
fool people into thinking you have made gold …

Making gold the easy way

1. Take a small piece of gold.

2. Heat some lead in a metal dish over a flame until it melts.

3. Drop the piece of gold into the melted lead and leave it to cool.

4. Gather together some rich people – the richer the better.

5. Place the lead-gold mixture over a flame. Take some powder
chalk, flour or pepper. Tell your audience, 'This is Powder of Elixir'
and sprinkle it on the hot lead.

6. Keep heating the dish till the lead boils away.

7. All that's left in the bottom of the dish is the gold.

8. Show your audience the gold and say, 'See! My Powder of Elixir
has turned the lead into gold!'

9. Sell your Powder of Elixir to the rich people.

10. Take your scrap of gold and take their gold coins.

Go as far away as possible before they find out that they've been tricked. And the experiment has worked. You really HAVE made yourself a lot of gold!

The magical mirror

Queen Elizabeth I's Wizard, John Dee (1527–1608), said he could look into the future using a 'speculum' – a magical mirror. You can test it for yourself. How?

a) There is always one marble in a bag of marbles that is really a small speculum.

b) Buy your own speculum from www.i'm-a-witch-get-me-out-of-here.co.uk for just £10,000.

c) See Dr. Dee's speculum in the British museum in London.

Answer: c) Dr. Dee was such a famous magician in the 1550s that Queen Elizabeth I went to him so he could tell her fortune ... even though Elizabeth had laws that banned fortune-telling! She also asked Dee to look into the stars and find the best day for her coronation.[10]

Elizabeth gave him a job in a college in Manchester – the students hated him. After Elizabeth died his house was wrecked and his books destroyed. He died poor ... which is better than dying hanged.

Mouse act

In England in the 1650s, a magician put on a witch act with the help of a mouse. How did he get the mouse to do what he said?

a) It was a clockwork mouse.

b) It was a stuffed mouse with a spring inside.

c) It was a live mouse that he trained using cheese.

10 You don't need the stars to tell you this. Monday is the best day. Nobody likes going to work on a Monday. Give people the day off to go to your coronation and they will love you to bits.

Answer: b) The man was a juggler who thought that his audience expected him to have a spirit to help him. He stuffed the skin of a mouse and stuck a coiled spring in the rear end. With practice he could drop it on the table, let it bounce twice and then catch it again.

He would put it into his pocket and tell it not to run away again as he needed it to help him do more tricks. From time to time he would make squeaky noises with his lips, pretending it was the mouse speaking like an imp.

The last witch

In the 1940s, Britain was at war with Germany. The Brits were terrified that the enemy would learn their secret plans. Posters went up all around the country...

At that time, in Portsmouth, Helen Duncan was a 'medium' … she said she could speak to spirits of the dead.

In 1944 Duncan said she had spoken to the spirit of a sailor who had been killed on HMS *Barham* in 1943.

The ship was a secret ship. No one should have known about it. The public didn't know the ship had been sunk. So how did Helen Duncan know?

They arrested her for being a 'vagrant' (a tramp).

But they couldn't lock her away and shut her up for that — they could only fine her 25p.

She wasn't a spy so they couldn't lock her up for that. It was a problem for the authorities.

They used the old laws from 1735:

Helen was shocked and said...

I never heard so many lies in my life.

It was said that Brit war-leader Winston Churchill believed in Helen's power to speak to the dead. Churchill finally scrapped the witchcraft law in 1951.

Helen Duncan, the last witch, died five years later.

Epilogue

For thousands of years people have killed those who performed magic.

Some 'witches' really believed they had magic powers. They were mad.

But the people who picked on witches were madder. Look at the mad people of Pittenweem in Fife, Scotland. Were they out of their minds? Here's what they did – decide for yourself.

In 1704, Janet Cornfoot was tried as a witch. She was tortured:

- Janet was locked in the church steeple but escaped.
- A mob from Pittenween caught her and beat her.
- They hung her up so they could pelt her with stones.
- They lay her on the ground and laid a heavy door on her.
- They piled stones on the door till she was crushed.
- They took out the body and drove a horse and cart over it.

The people of Pittenweem were never punished.

That's horrible history for you.

Do you still believe witches are just funny old ladies with pointy hats and broomsticks?

There are still a few people today who call themselves witches, and they will probably be upset to read that there is no such thing as witchcraft.

They may even try to put a curse on me.

Do I care?

No, I don't. All I have to say to them is....

NOTE FROM THE EDITOR

We are sorry this book was not quite finished. Mr Deary went missing while working on the last page. Police say the only clue is the frog they found sitting in his chair.

Interesting Index

Hang on! This isn't one of your boring old indexes. This is a horrible index. It's the only index in the world where you will find 'nose-picking', 'flesh-eating lice', 'snail juice' and all the other things you really HAVE to know if you want to be a horrible historian. Read it and creep.